JAZZ WARM-UPS
FOR GUITAR

BY MICHAEL ANTHONY

To Access the Online Audio Go to:
www.melbay.com/21103BCDEB

© 2006 BY MEL BAY PUBLICATIONS, INC., PACIFIC, MO 63069
ALL RIGHTS RESERVED. INTERNATIONAL COPYRIGHT SECURED. B.M.I. MADE AND PRINTED IN U.S.A.
No part of this publication may be reproduced in whole or in part, or in a retrieval system, or transmitted in any form
or by any means, electronic, mechanical, photocopy, recording, or otherwise, without the written permission of the publisher.
Visit us on the Web at www.melbay.com – E-mail us at email@melbay.com

Audio Contents

Title	Dur.	Track
Minor Patterns	2:30	1
Major Patterns	2:30	2
Super Arpeggio	1:15	3
Super Arpeggio-Groups of 3	:33	4
Super Arpeggio-Groups of 4	:33	5
Flamenco Right-Hand	:48	6
Am7 - D7 Arpeggio Study	:45	7
Am7b5 - D7b9 Arpeggio Study	:45	8
Dm7 - G7 Arpeggio Study	:45	9
Dm7b5 - G7b9 Arpeggio Study	:48	10
A7 - D7	1:20	11
C minor Be-Bop	1:18	12
Three String Major Pattern	:58	13
Four String Geometry	:53	14
Chromatic Geometry	:32	15

Title	Dur.	Track
Whole Tone Patterns	:56	16
Add a Note	:49	17
Arpeggio Study	:45	18
Thirds	:41	19
Fourths	:39	20
Etude In G Major	:29	21
Minor Etude	:40	22
Diminished Pattern	:27	23
I, VI, ii, V Etude	:46	24
F Minor Study	:44	25
Around The Circle	:35	26
Circle Variation	:33	27
G Minor Line Study	:35	28
Major Blues	:36	29
Minor Blues	:28	30

Contents

Acknowledgements	2
Introduction	3
Warm-Up #1	3
Warm-Up #2	4
Warm-Up #3	4
Warm-Up #4	5
Warm-Up #5	5
Warm-Up #6	6
Warm-Up #7-11	6
Warm-Up #12	7
Warm-Up #13	8
Warm-Up #14	9
Warm-Up #15	10
Warm-Up #16	11
Warm-Up #17	12
Warm-Up #18	14
Warm-Up #19	15
Warm-Up #20	17
Warm-Up #21	18
Warm-Up #22	19
Warm-Up #23	20
Warm-Up #24	21
Warm-Up #25	21
Warm-Up #26 & 27	22
Warm-Up #28	24
Warm-Up #29	25
Warm-Up #30	26
About the Author	28

Acknowledgements

- I would like to thank Robert Gish (an author in his own right) for helping to organize this text.
- I wish to thank my good friend Mitch Holder for introducing me to Bill Bay.
- The audio was recorded at CasaBlanca Prod., www.casablancaprod.net

Thirty Challenging Guitar Warm-Ups

Introduction

These warm-ups are intended for any guitarist willing to practice who wants to improve both right and left-hand dexterity. They are challenging, jazz-oriented exercises in concept and in execution and primarily most suitable for players at intermediate to advanced levels. I use these studies throughout my teaching—in university and secondary school jazz classes and in private lessons.

Some of these studies offer suggestions, including left-hand fingering, on how to play them though you are encouraged to experiment. Some are in 4/4 time but some are in odd meters like 6/4 and 10/4 to exploit a given position on the guitar.

Most of these studies involve a musical premise; however, some are based on a geometric shape. Remember too that correct practice and repetition will help assure mastery of these etudes and their application in your playing. Good luck and have fun.

Warm-Up 1

Good for both hands. Based off of the 1,2,3,5 degrees from F minor and continuing up in fourths (1,2,3,5 B♭ minor, etc). A two-string pattern, using five keys in one area of the guitar, reversing itself when descending, ending on F minor. Alternate picking advised at first with downstroke, then reverse, starting with upstroke. Then explore other possibilities. Move up and down in half or whole steps to the 9th or 10th position.

Warm-Up 2

This is a continuation of WU1 but is based on 1,2,3,5 degrees of a major chord. You may stretch between finger one and two (preferred) or three and four.

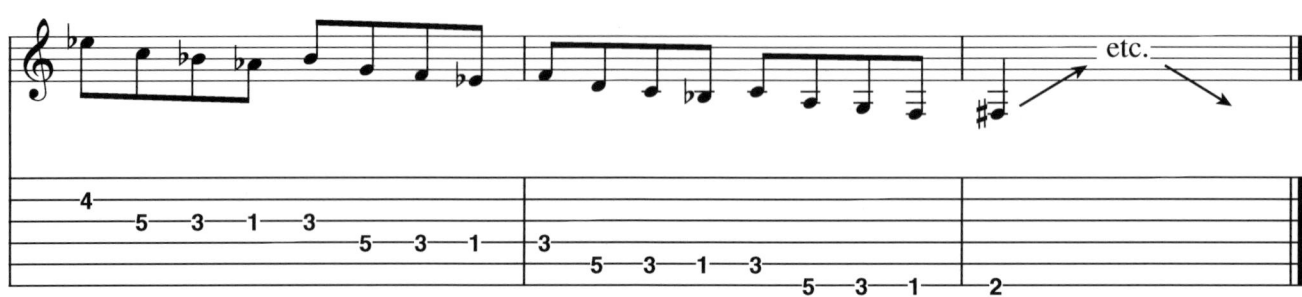

Warm-Up 3

My students call this the "Super Arpeggio." It is based on thirds on a diatonic scale in one position. In the low position it's a D♭ with F as the lowest note. Practice at first by repeating the first two bars. This exercise is movable and thus should be practiced in other keys. The second level of practice involves playing the first two bars ascending chromatically and then descending. Diatonically these can be worked out for every degree of the scale and are equally sonorous.

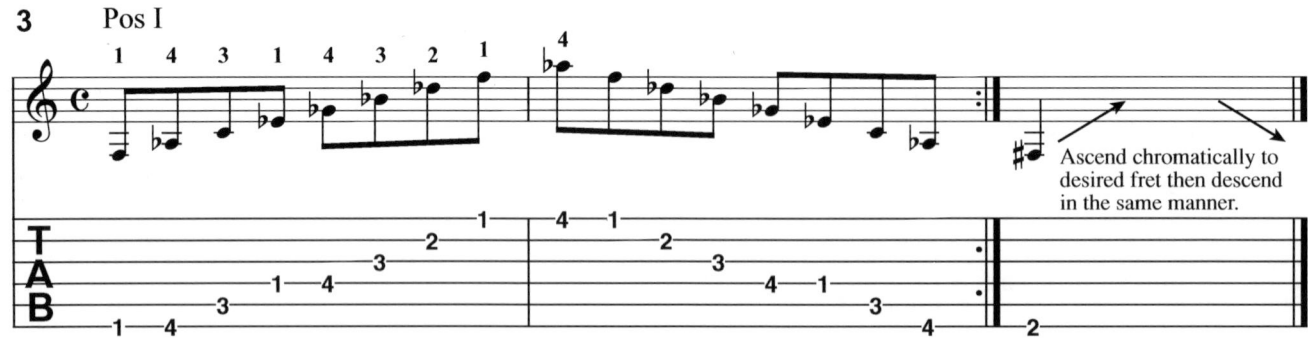

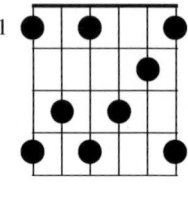

4

Warm-Up 4

This exercise, excellent for developing technique in both hands, is built off of WU3 but is in the fifth position (the key of F). Play the pattern in groups of three.

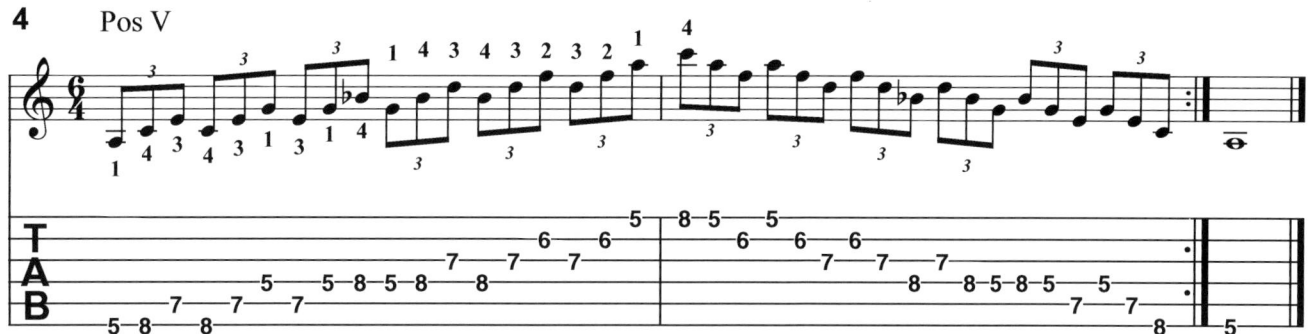

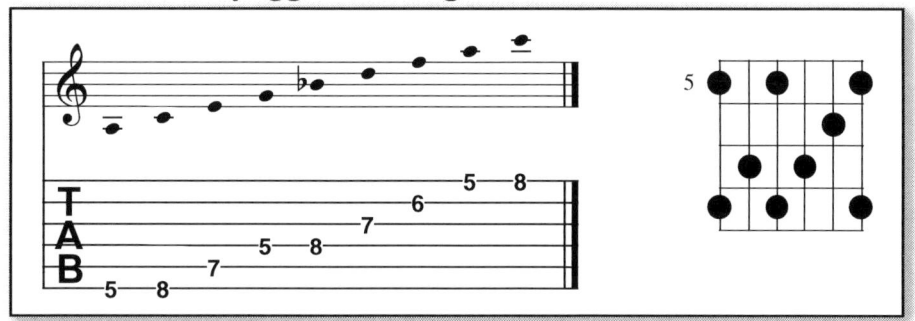

Warm-Up 5

This is a further development of WU4 in groups of four.

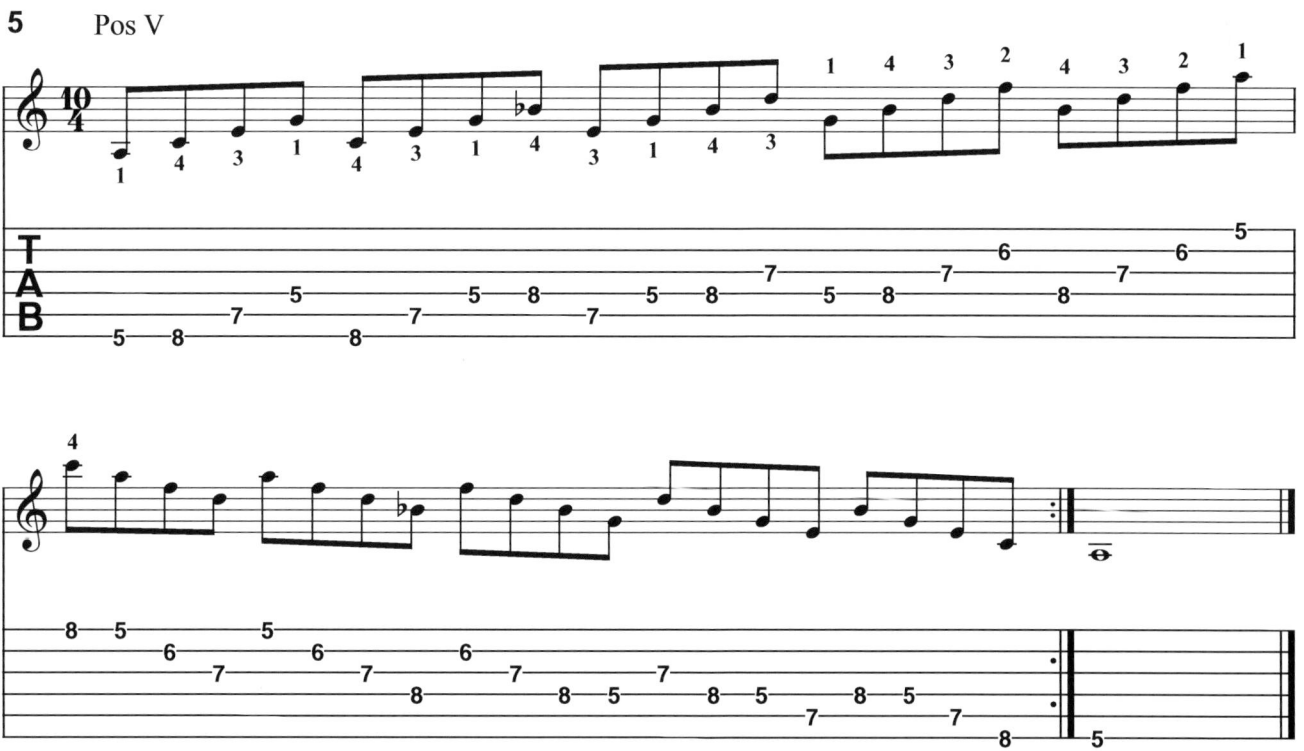

Warm-Up 6

This exercise bears a flamenco influence and is equally rewarding for right-hand technique with fingers or pick.

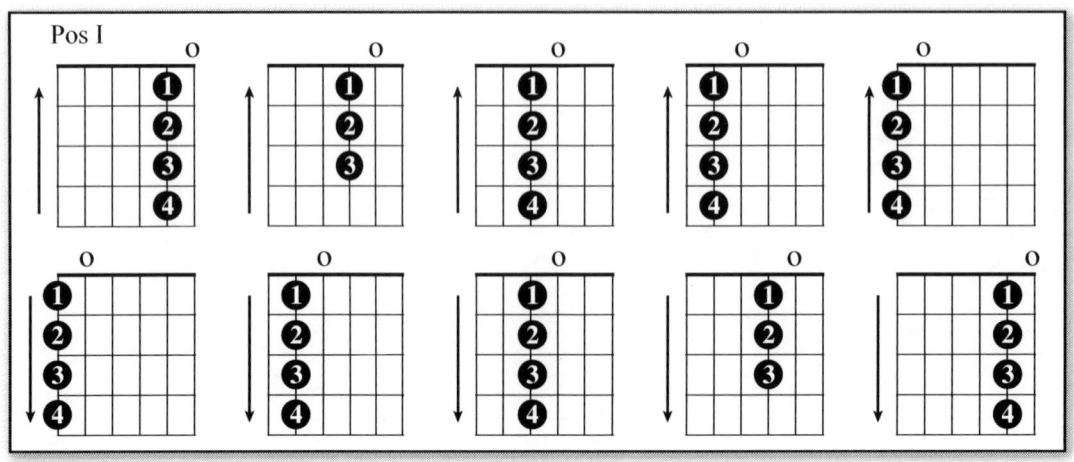

Diagram for #6

Warm-ups 7-11

Movement here is up and down in half steps. They may be sequenced as warm-ups 7-9; 8-10 or in parallel order. Numbers 7-10 are ii-V progressions, while number 11 is a Dominant 7 exercise.

#7 through #11 – Move up and down in whole or half steps

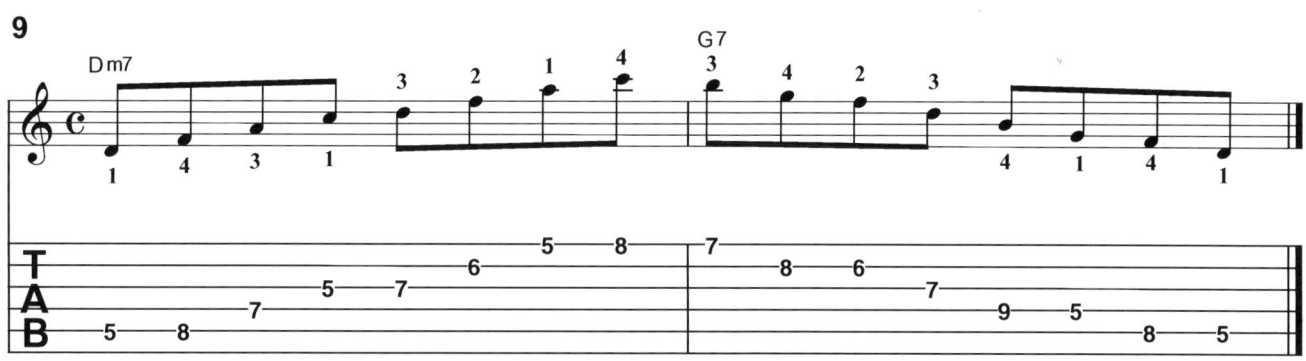

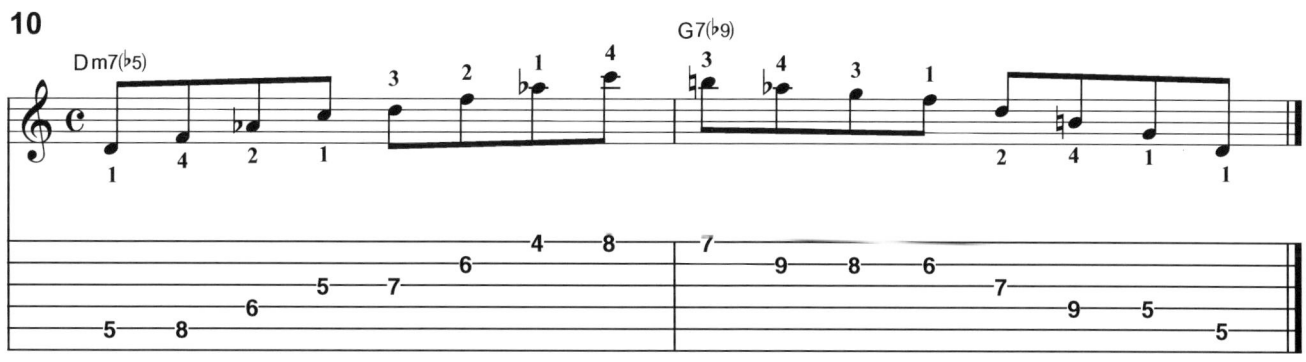

7

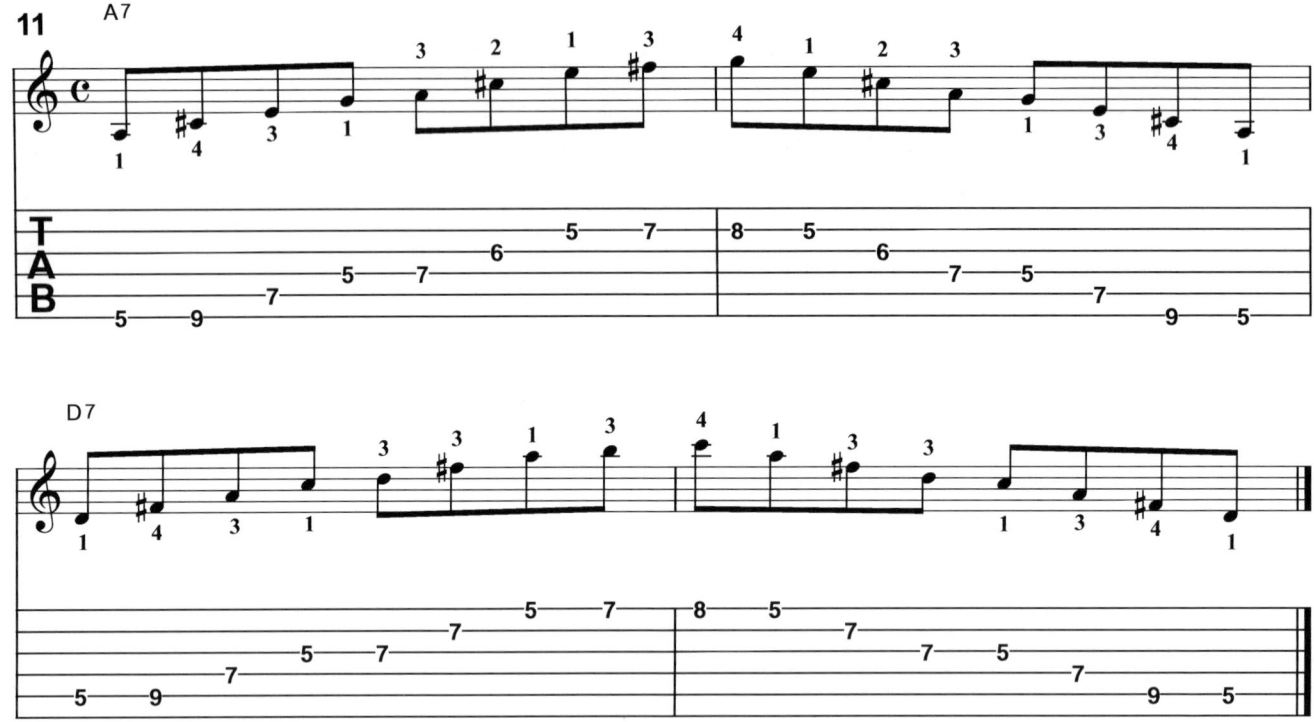

Warm-up 12

This etude is based on two bebop licks and may repeat continuously in one key up or down in whole steps.

Warm-up 13

13 3-String Pattern with Major Triads

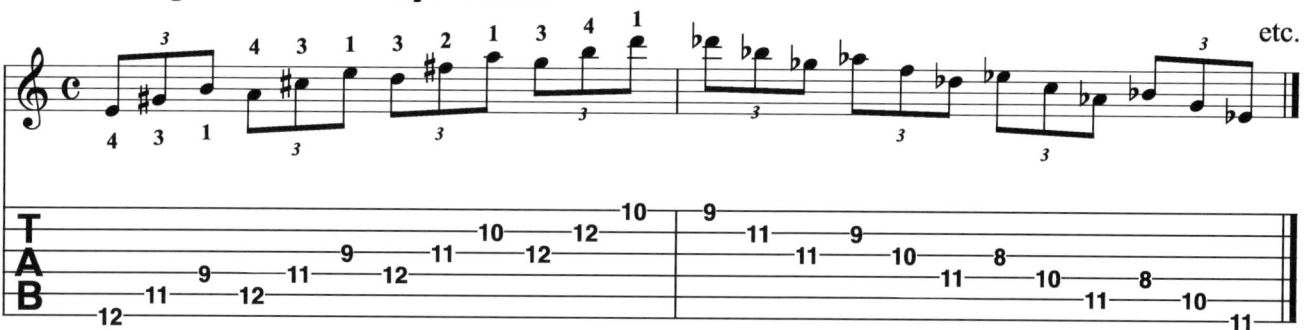

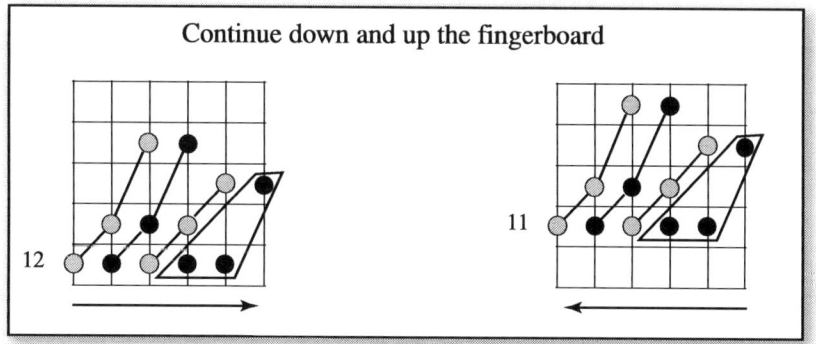

Continue down and up the fingerboard

Warm-up 14

14 Geometric 4-String Pattern

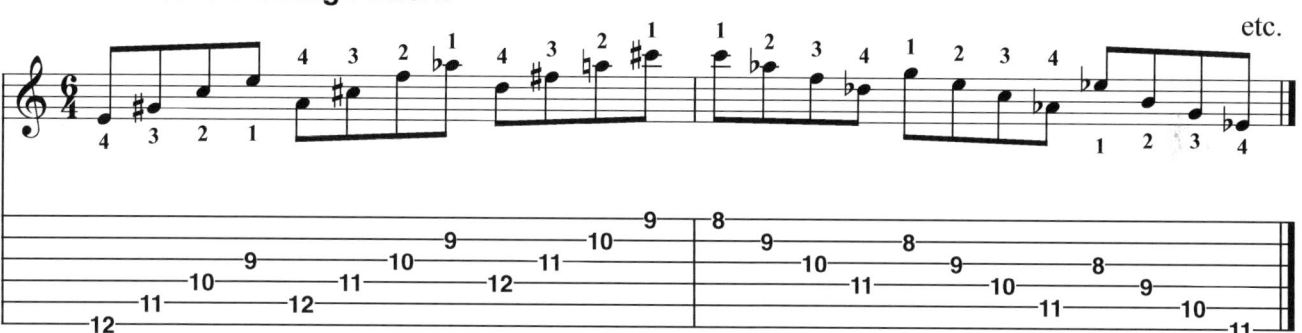

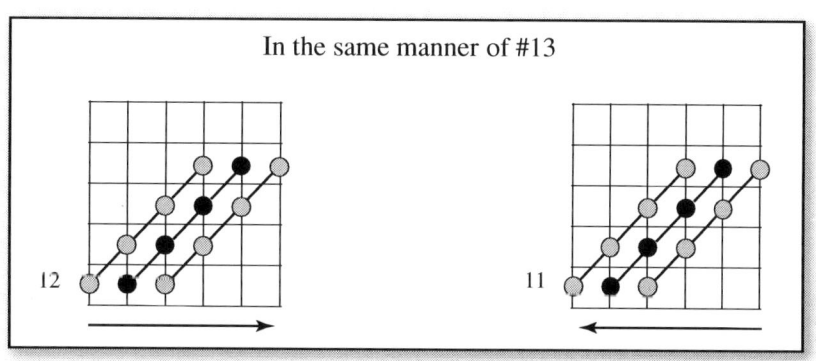

In the same manner of #13

Warm-up 15

Another flamenco pattern handed down as a speed drill, based here on both chromatic an geometric patterns.

Warm-Up 16

Patterns based on the whole tone scale. Each one can be practiced individually or may be connected.

16 A Whole Tone Patterns

Warm-Up 17

This may be referred to as "add a note" and is based on the C major scale. Play the first notes of the scale and then return to the first note and continue up, adding a note as you go. This may apply to other forms, using the principle of ascending movement. Next step is to apply the principle in descending order.

17 Add-a-Note

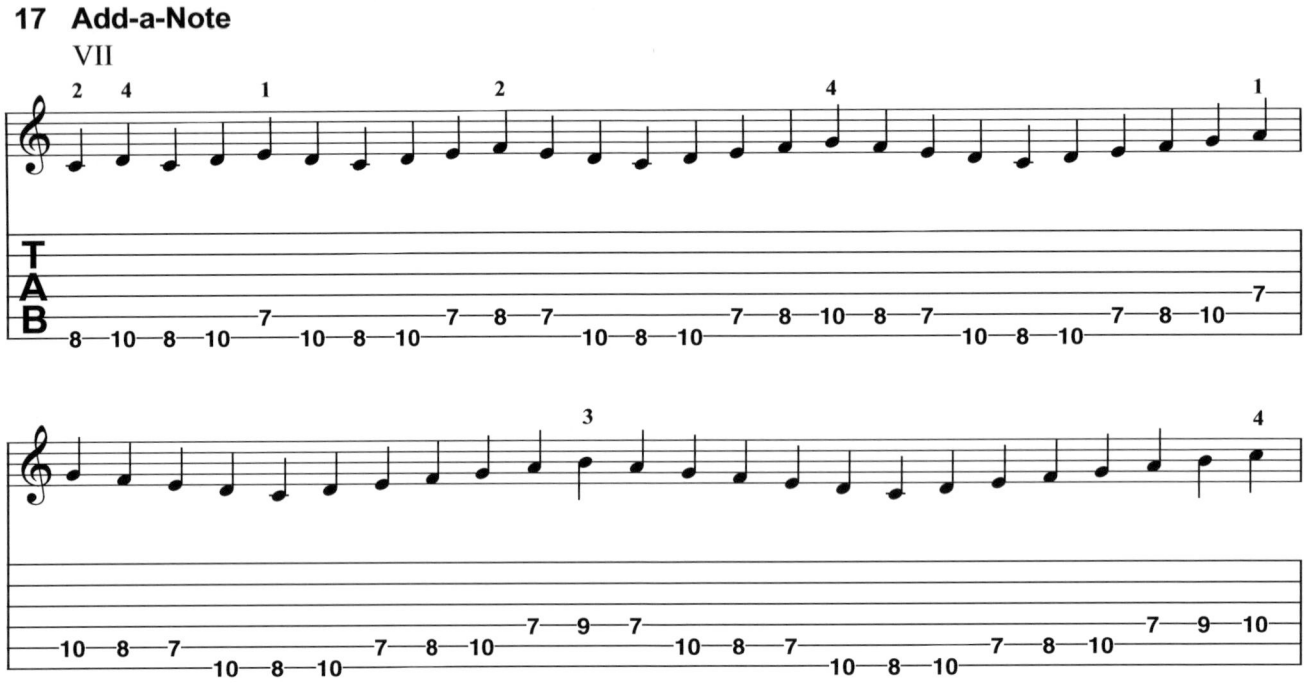

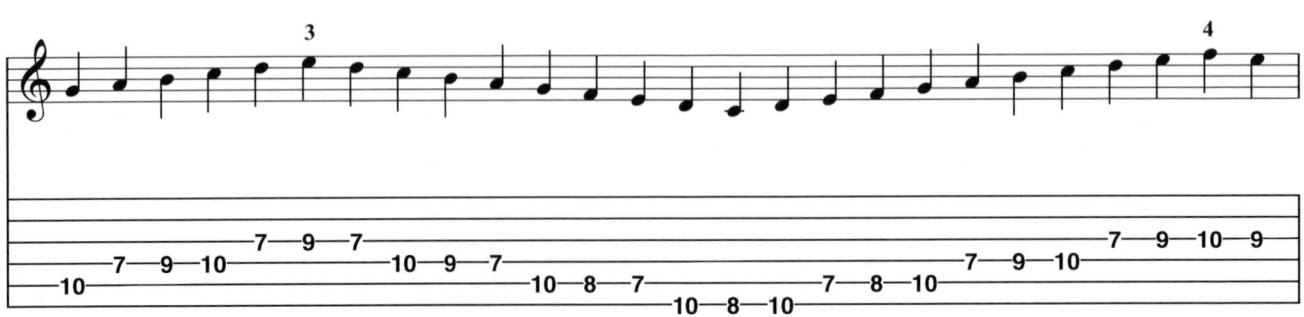

12

17 Cont'd

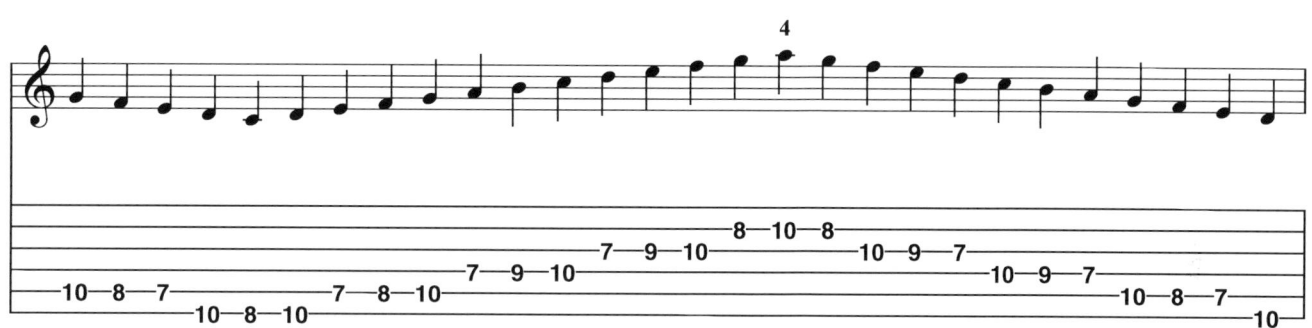

Scale and Diagram for #17
C Major

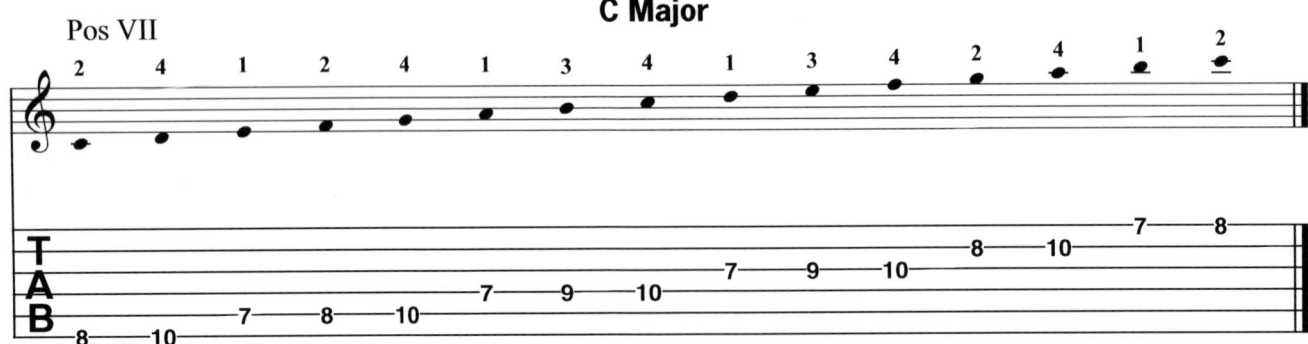

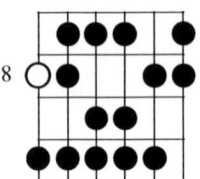

Warm-Up 18

These are basic arpeggio forms in the key of G with the added seventh. This is a parallel arpeggio etude. Each one of these may be practiced individually first, then as written.

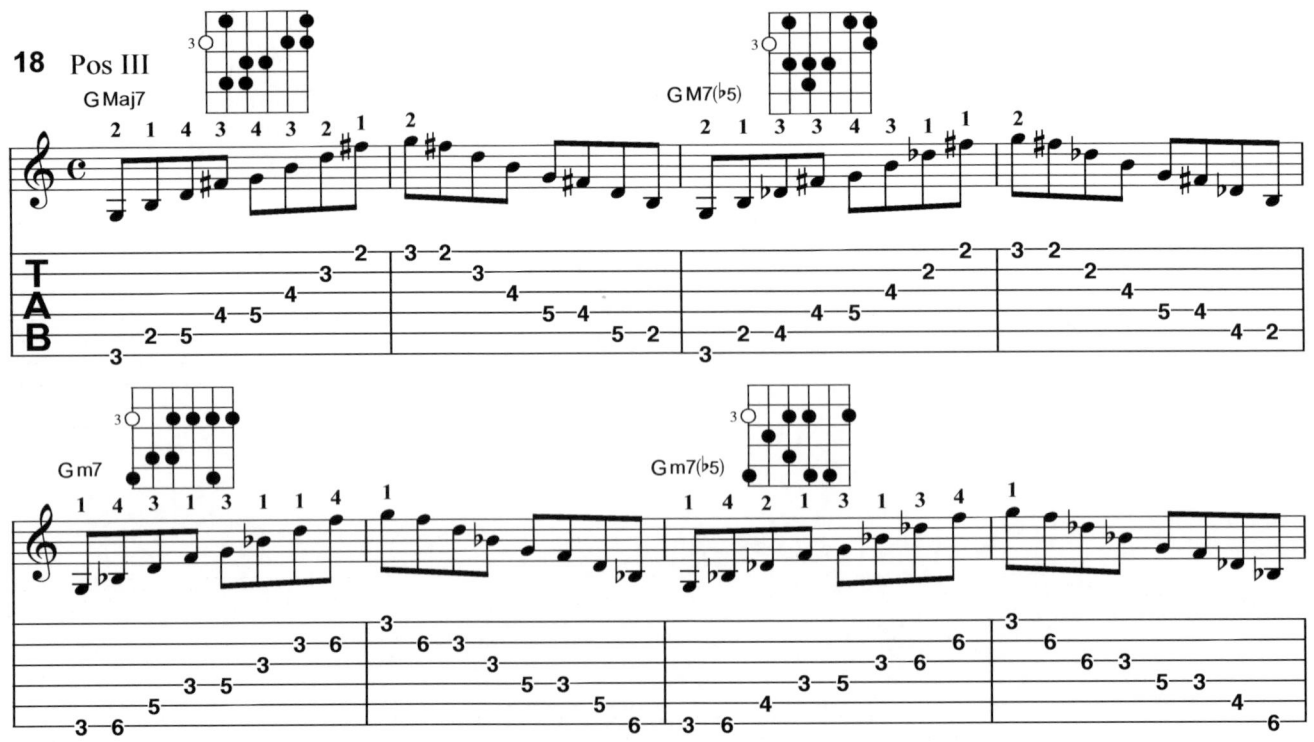

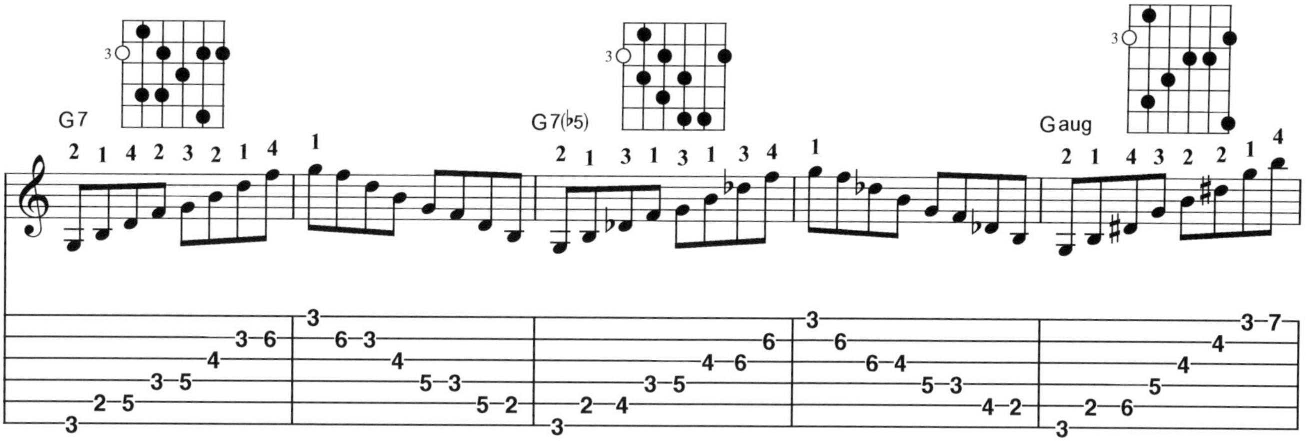

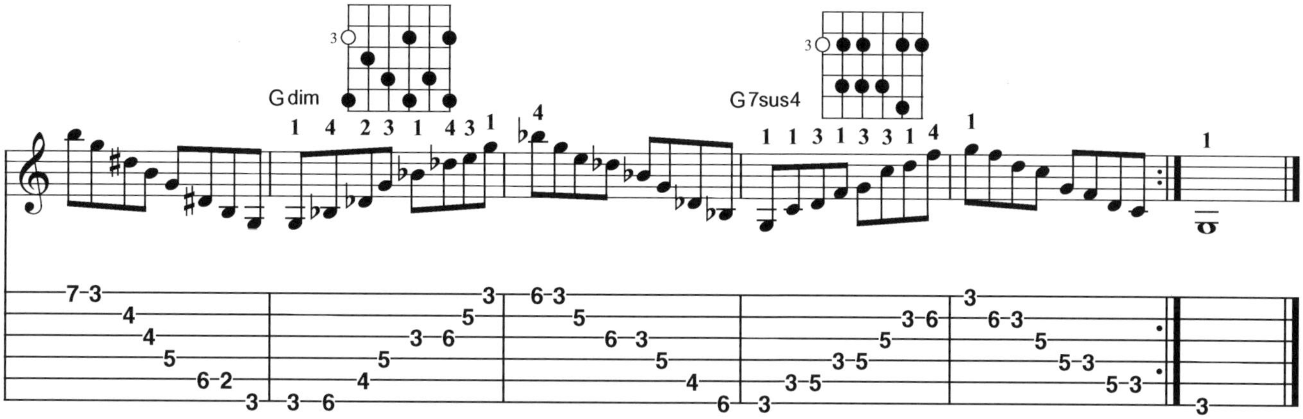

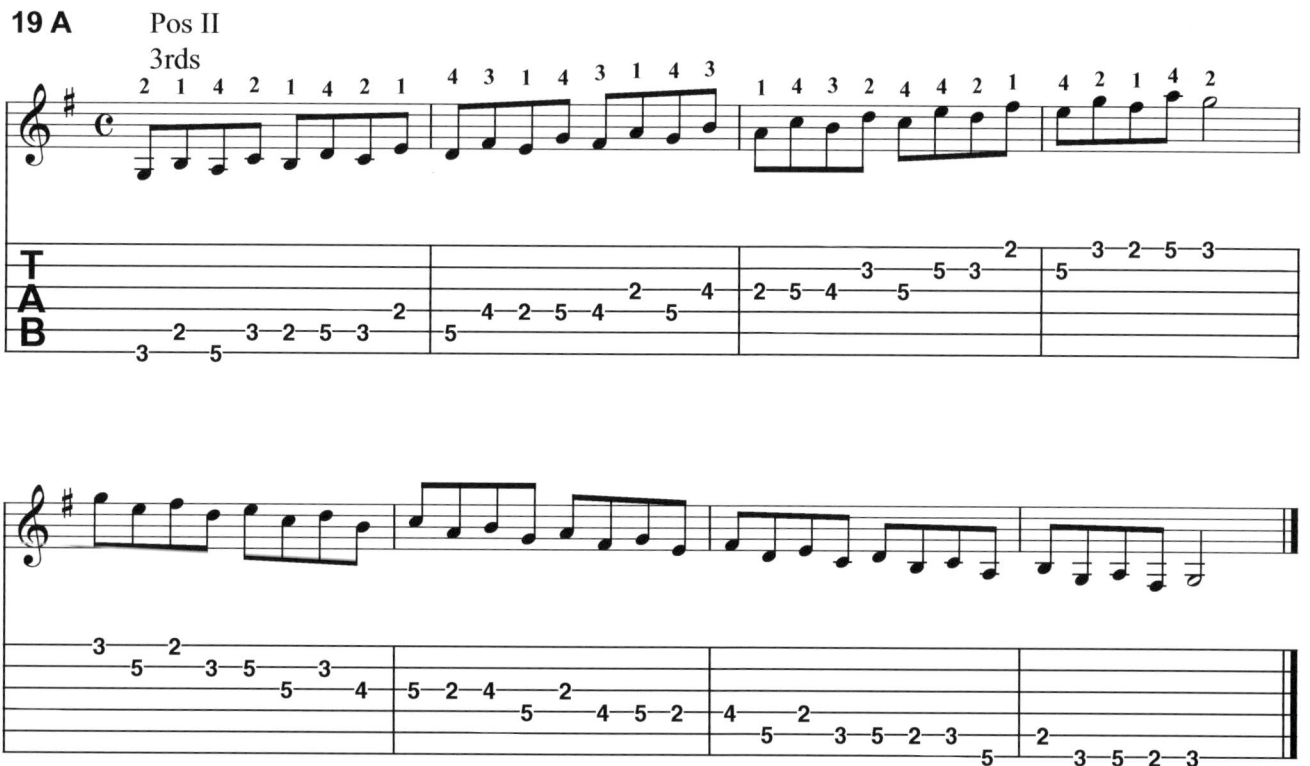

Warm-Up 19

Etudes in thirds. May be practiced individually or connected. Nineteen B is the inversion of nineteen A.

19 A Pos II

3rds

19 B

Scale and Diagram for #19 A and B
G Major

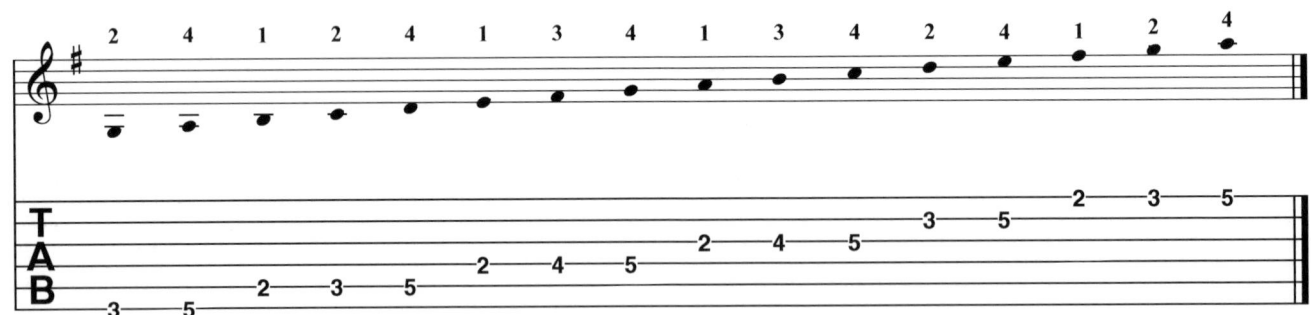

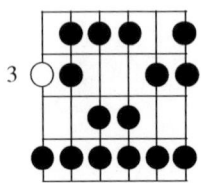

Warm-Up 20

Same idea as number nineteen, only this deals with intervals of fourths.

Scale and Diagram for #20 A and B
G Dorian (Gm7)

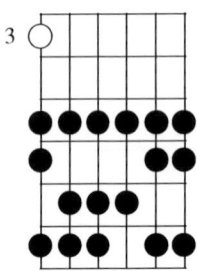

Warm-Up 21

Gmaj 7 to C-7, I to IV minor etude; triplets challenging especially in the second part.

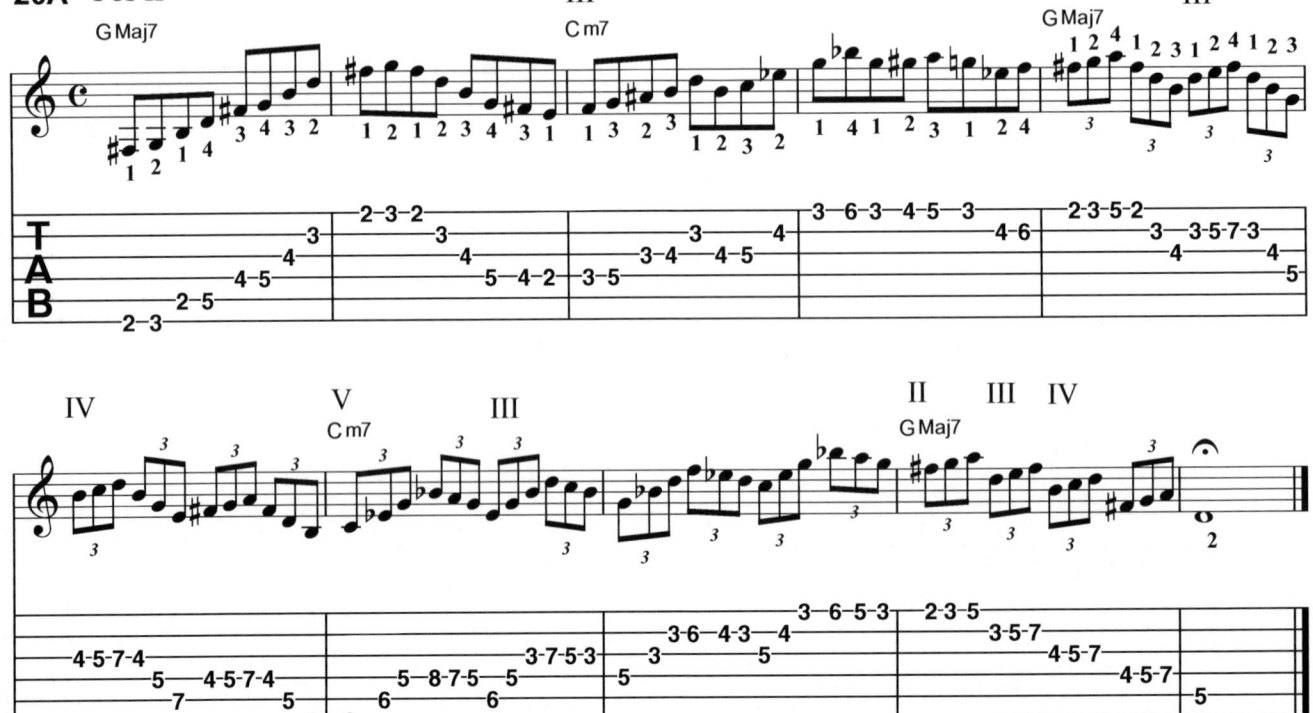

Warm-Up 22

A standard minor progression. Here on the first set of four strings. Works down in whole steps in three keys (similar to "This Masquerade" progression).

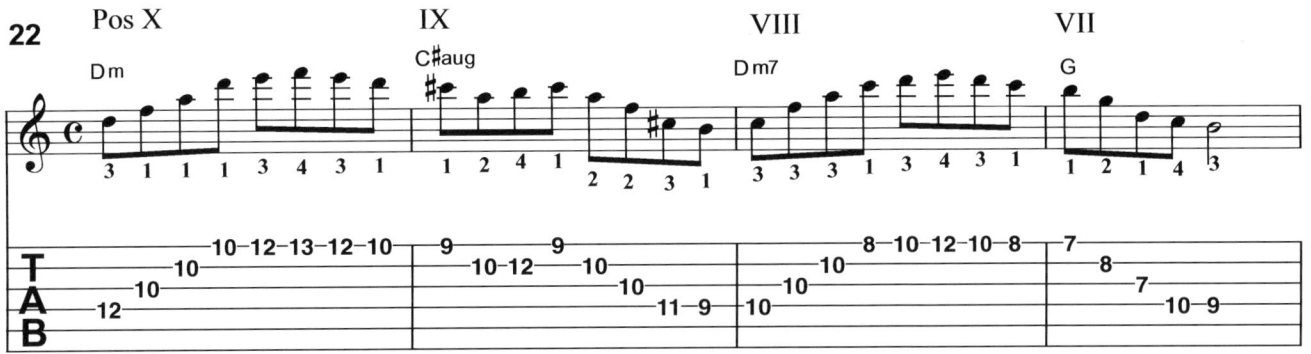

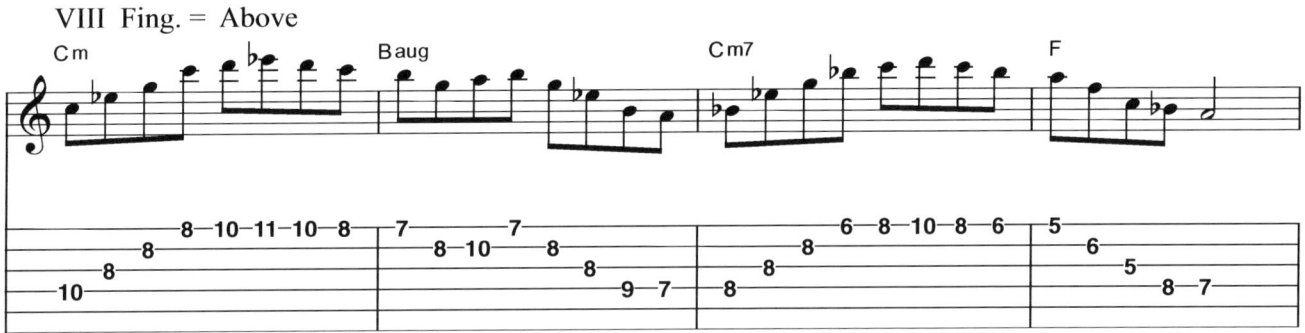

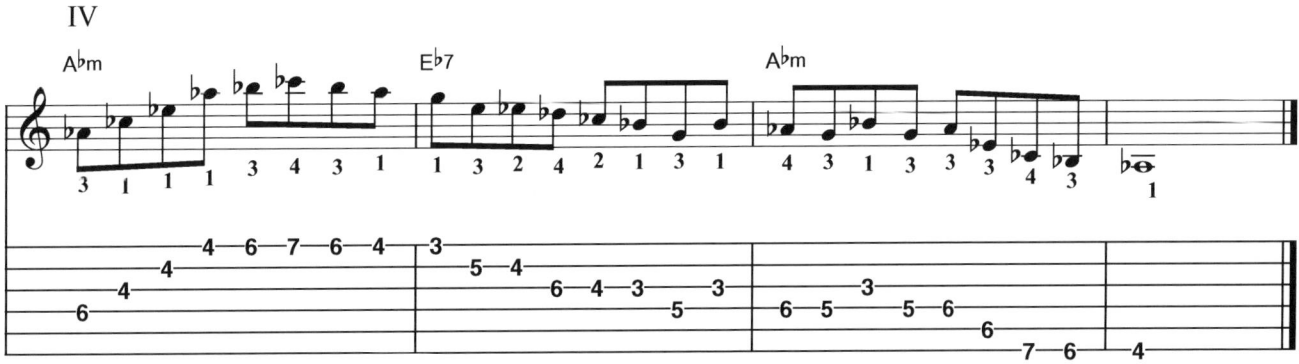

Warm-Up 23

Dominant 7 arpeggios, ascending and descending in minor thirds which spells out a diminished scale; good for both left and right hand.

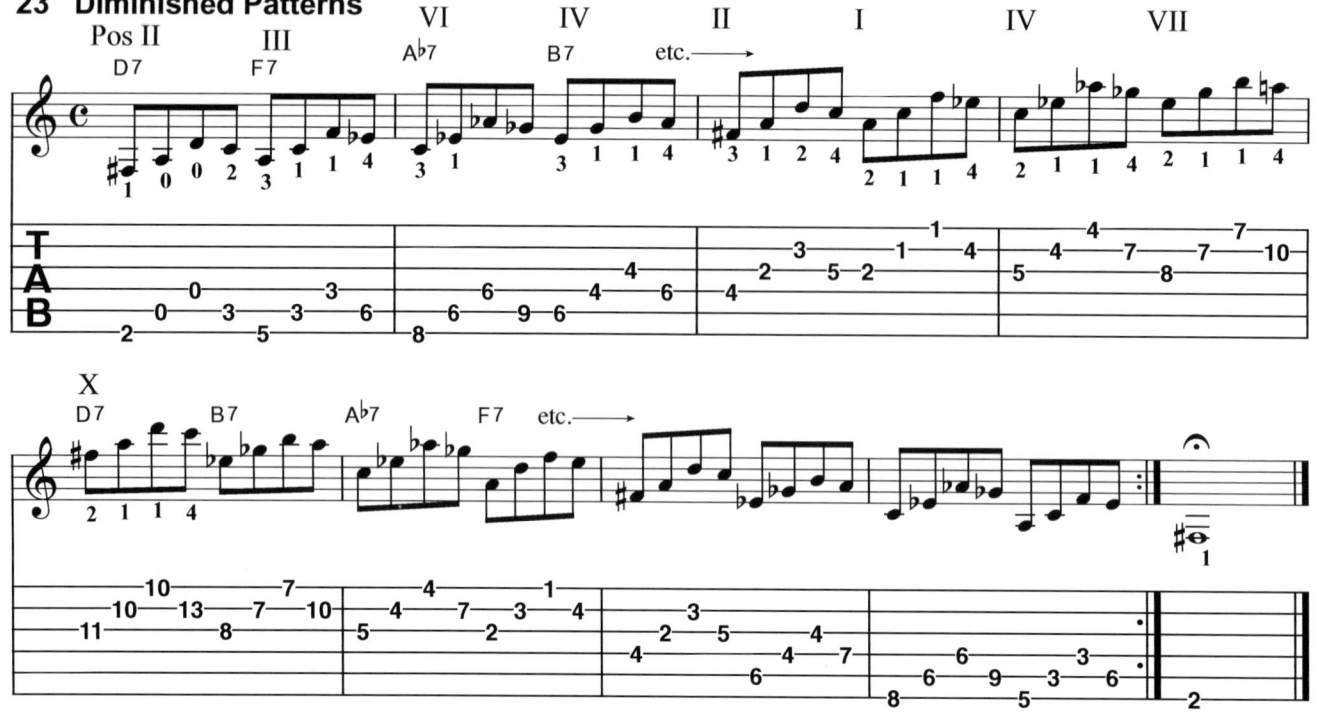

Warm-Up 24

Line study on I, VI, ii, V progression in major with the line moving up in minor thirds.

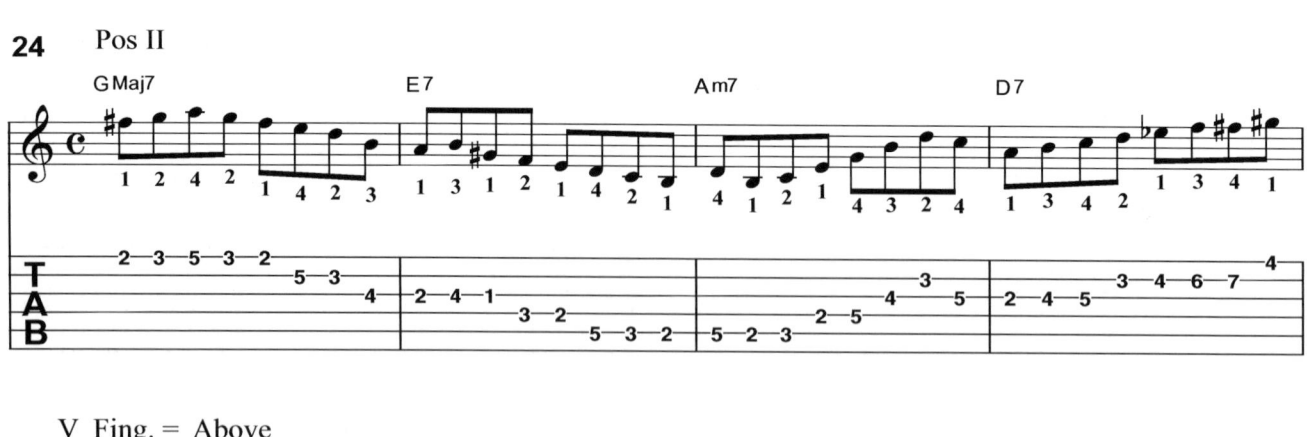

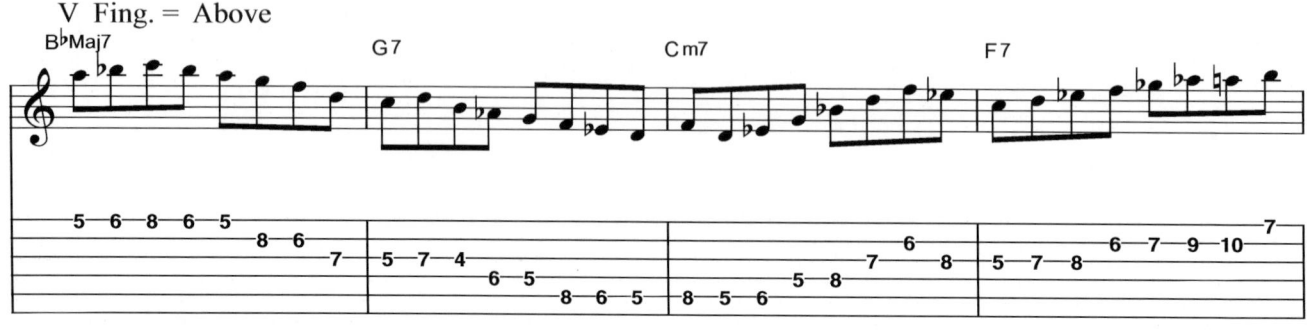

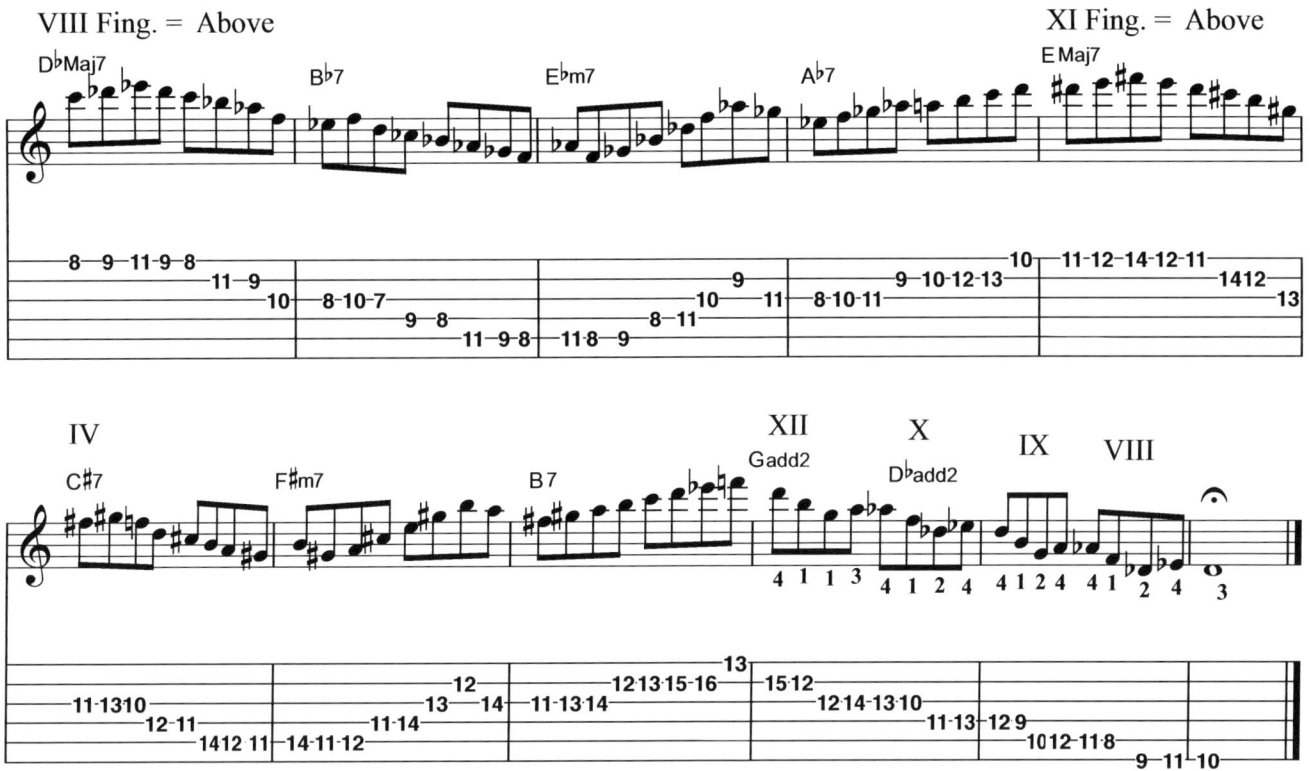

Warm-Up 25

F minor 7 pattern from bottom to top, top to bottom, the entire length of the fingerboard. Bars 1-8 in the same pattern ascending up the root third and fifth of the chord. Bar 9 begins a new pattern for the descent.

25 Fm Study

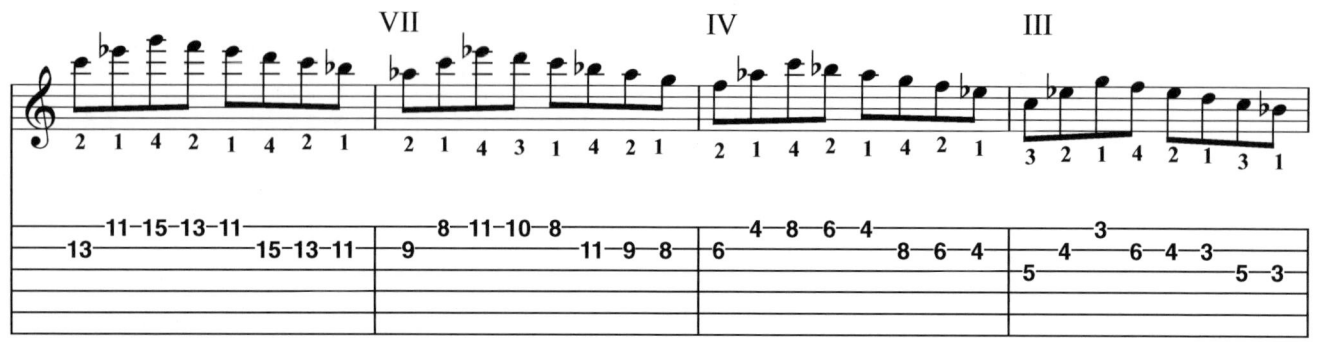

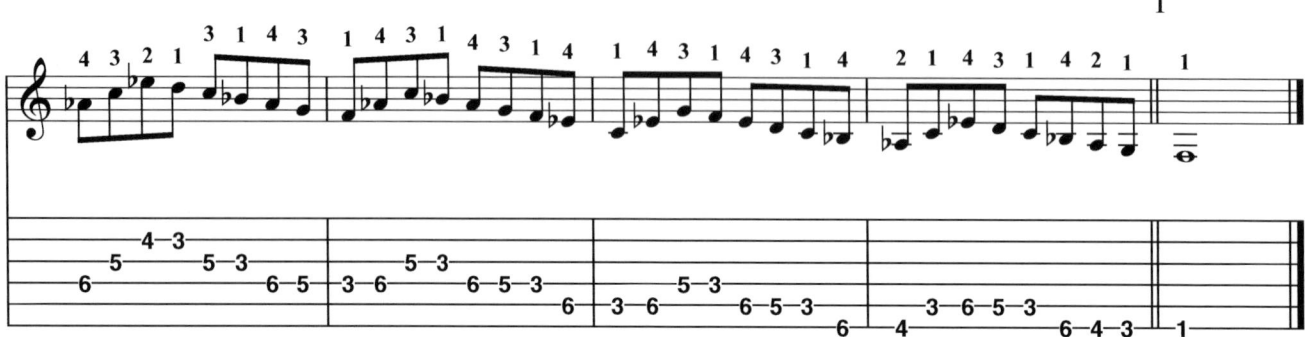

Warm-Ups 26 and 27

Circle of 4ths and 5ths down the neck. Begins with C Dom 7 upward, one bar each. These may hook up with each other.

26 Circle of 4th and 5th Down the Neck

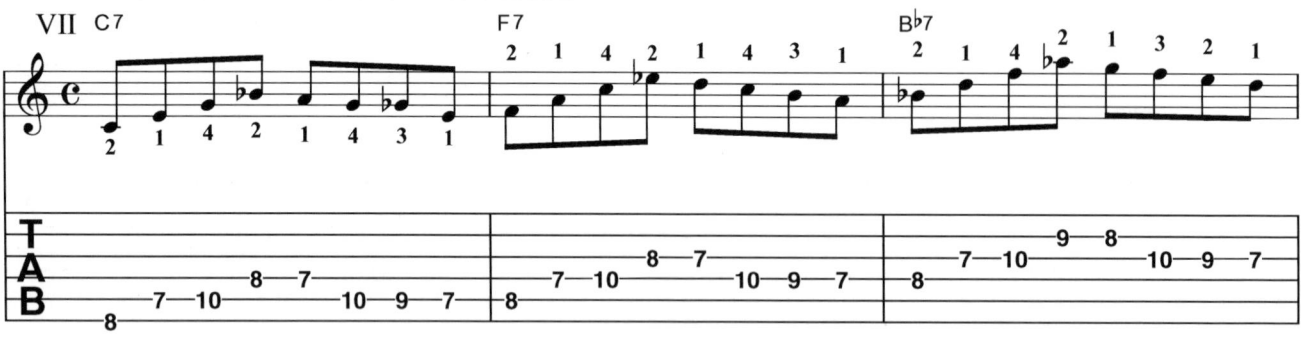

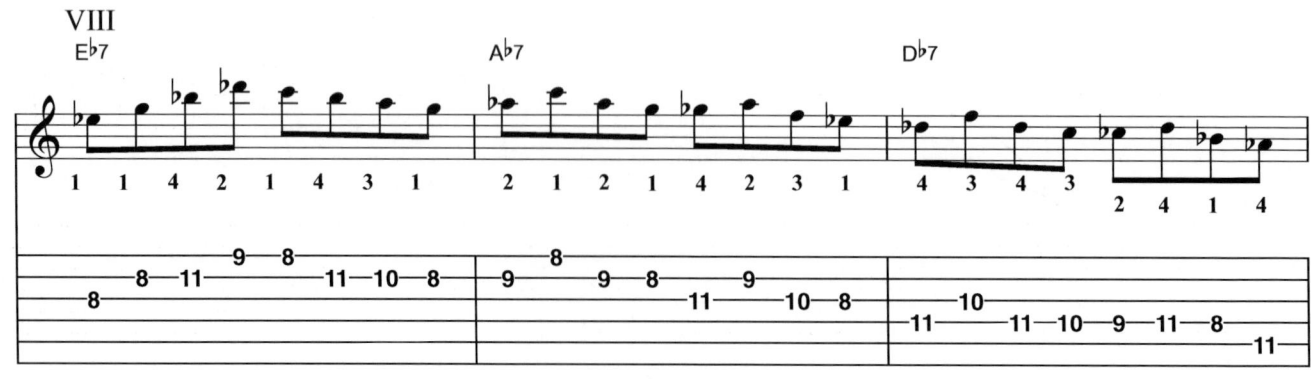

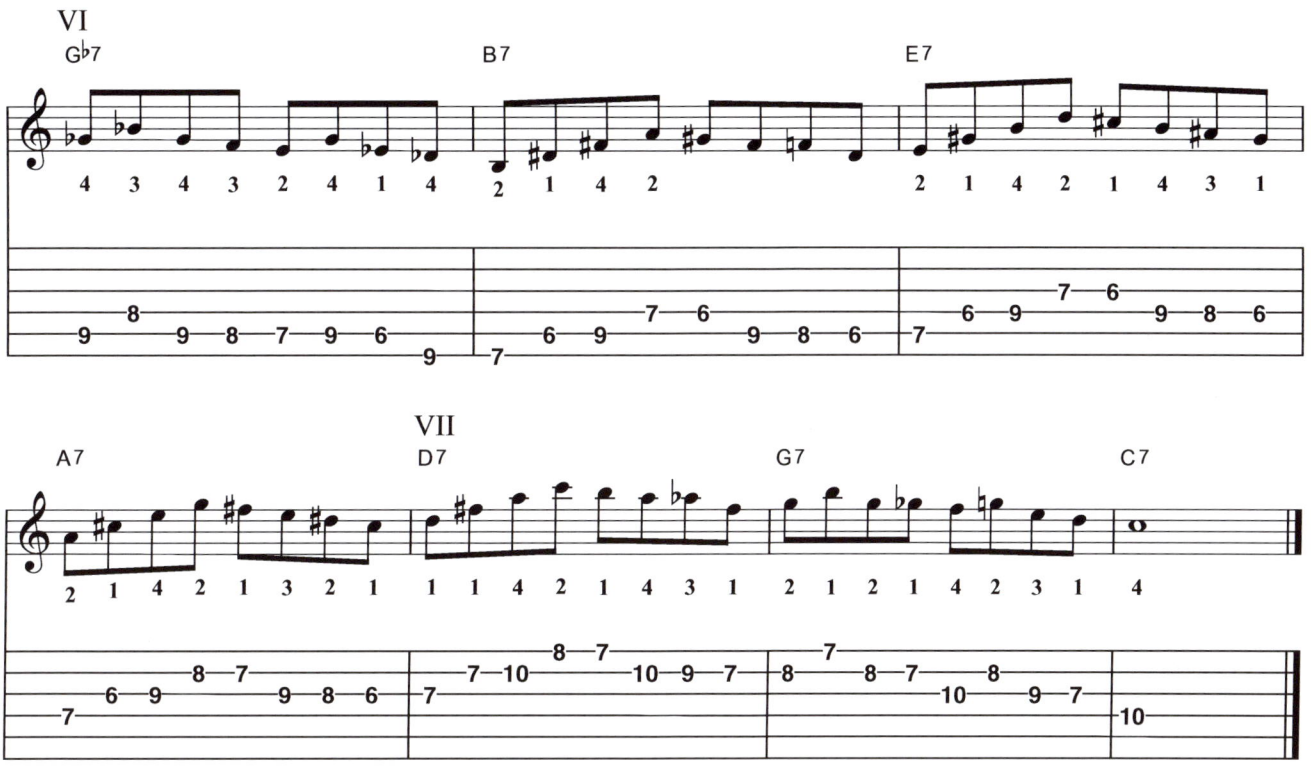

27 Circle of 4th and 5th Up the Neck

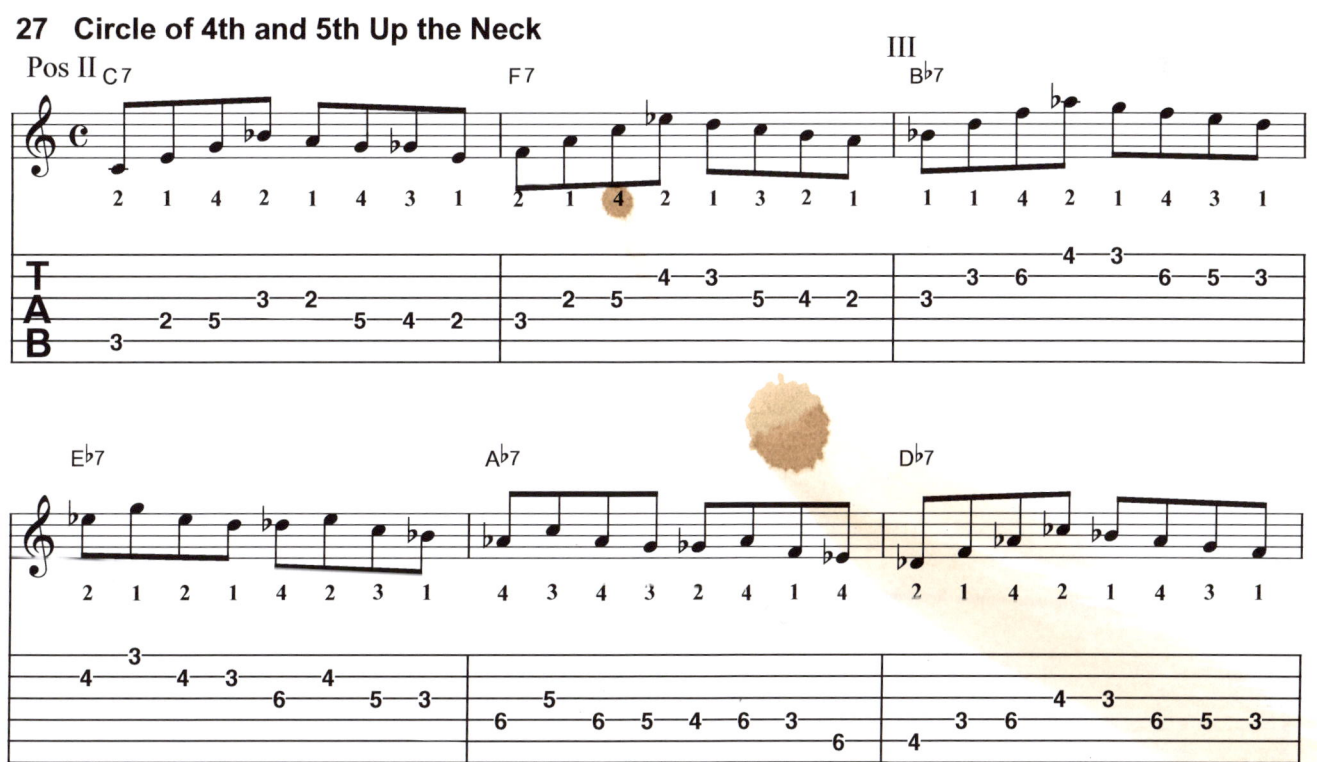

Warm-Up 28

Line study on I, VI, ii, V progression in G minor, using the five basic scale forms.

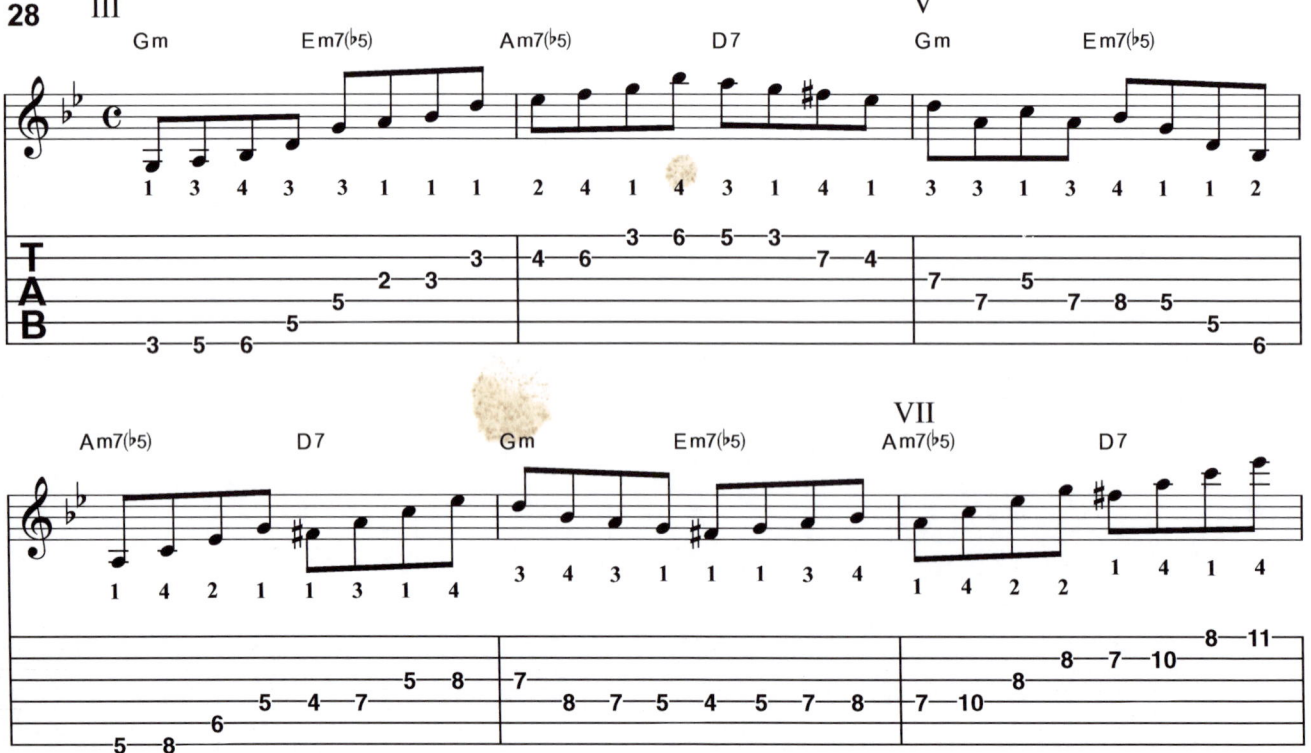

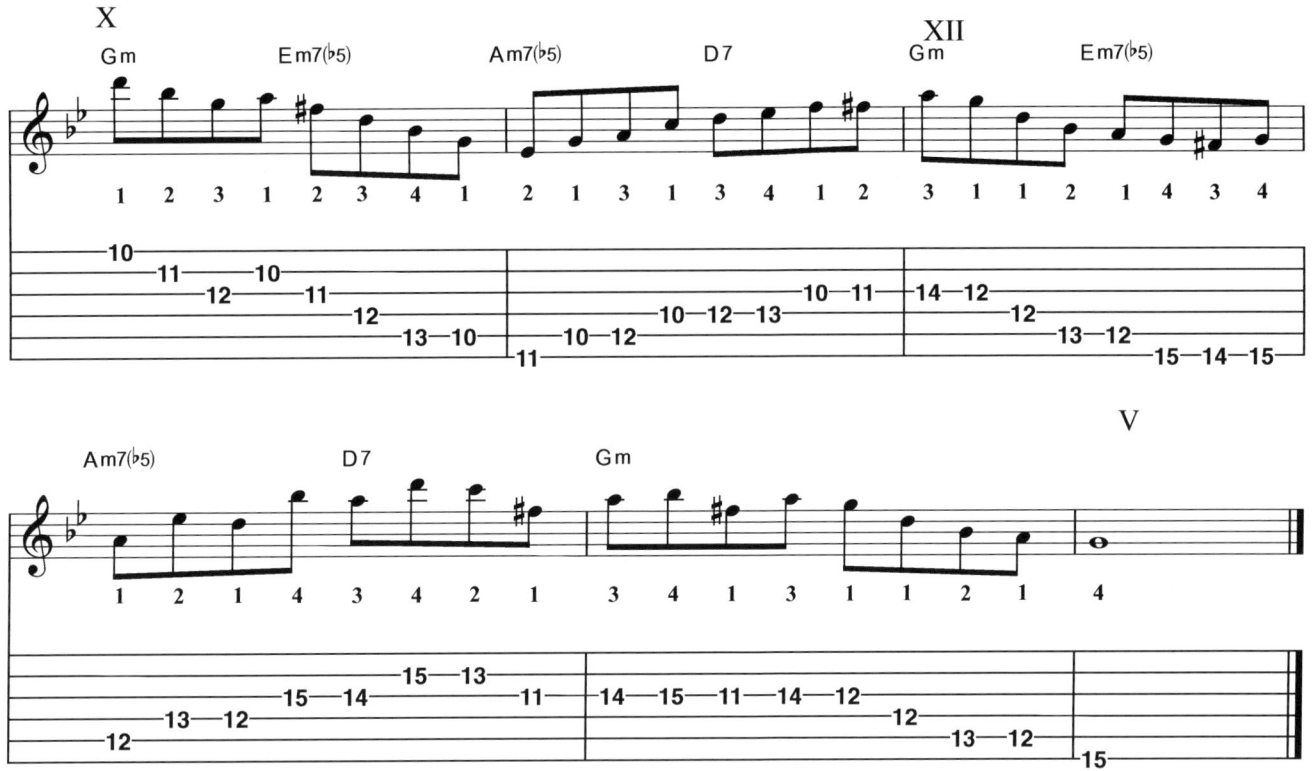

Warm-Up 29

Line study on C major blues, using the tri-tone principle (first bar is C arpeggio, shifting to G♭ major arpeggio); bars 5 and 6 use the same principle as the first bar. Bars seven and eight the line is patterned around Em7 shifting to E♭7. Bar ten melodic pattern is a tri-tone (diminished fifth) above the Dm7. Bar 12, beats 3 and 4 is a descending line using the tri-tone interval.

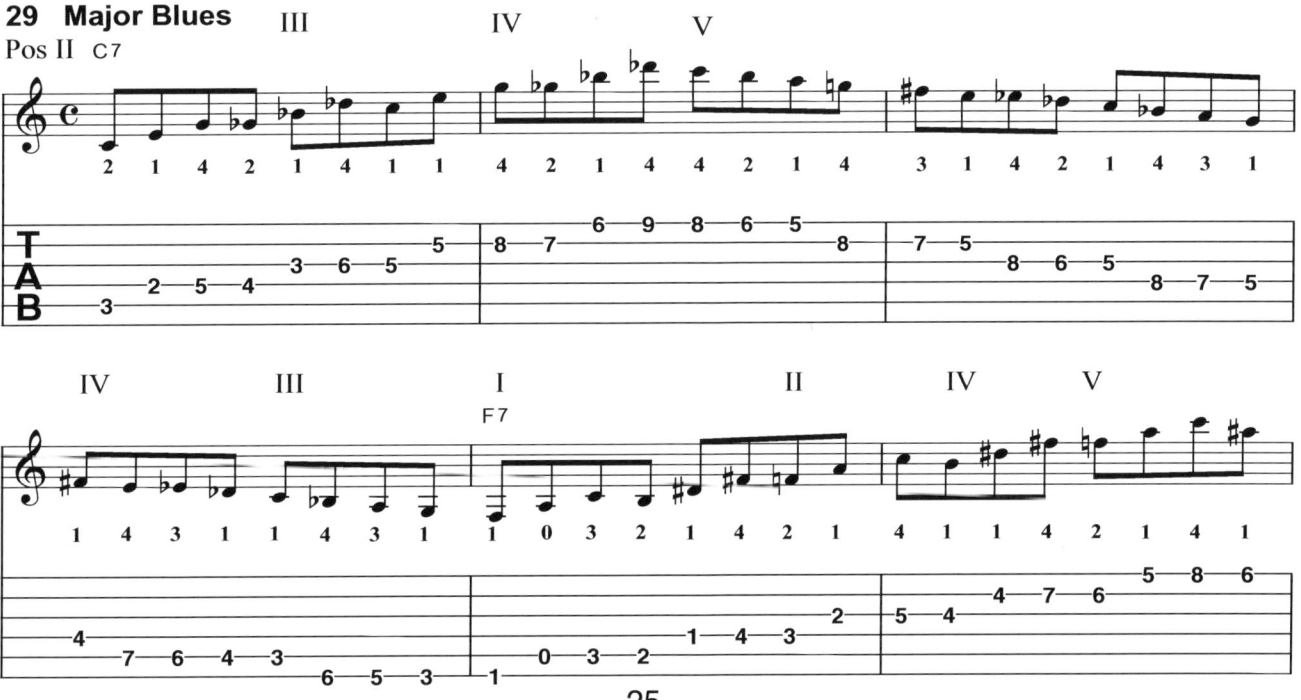

25

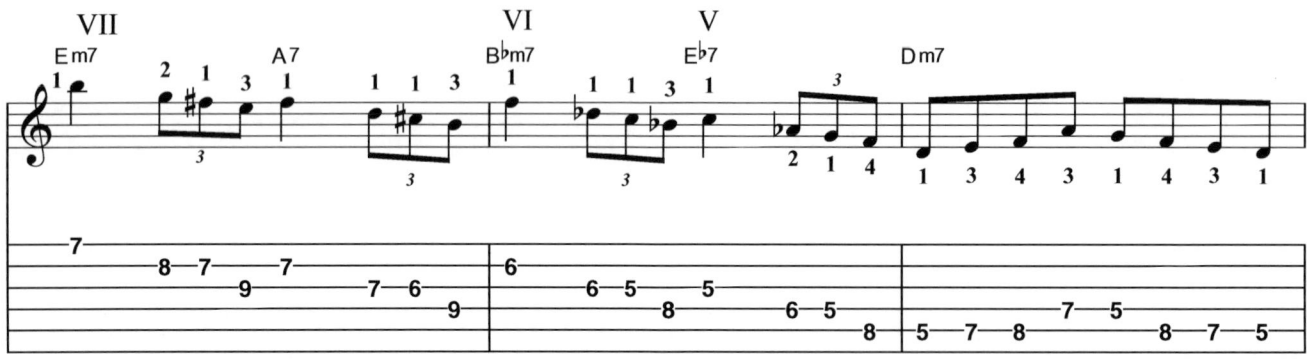

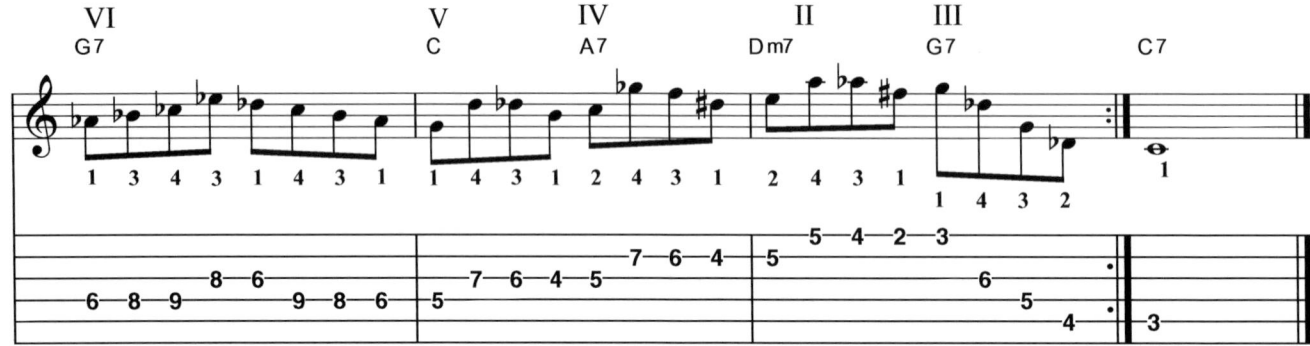

Warm-Up 30

A line study C minor Blues etude.

29 Minor Blues

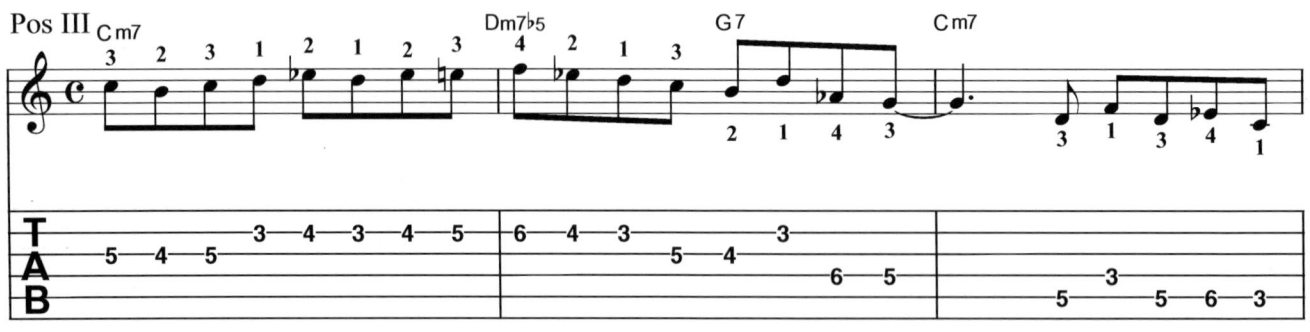

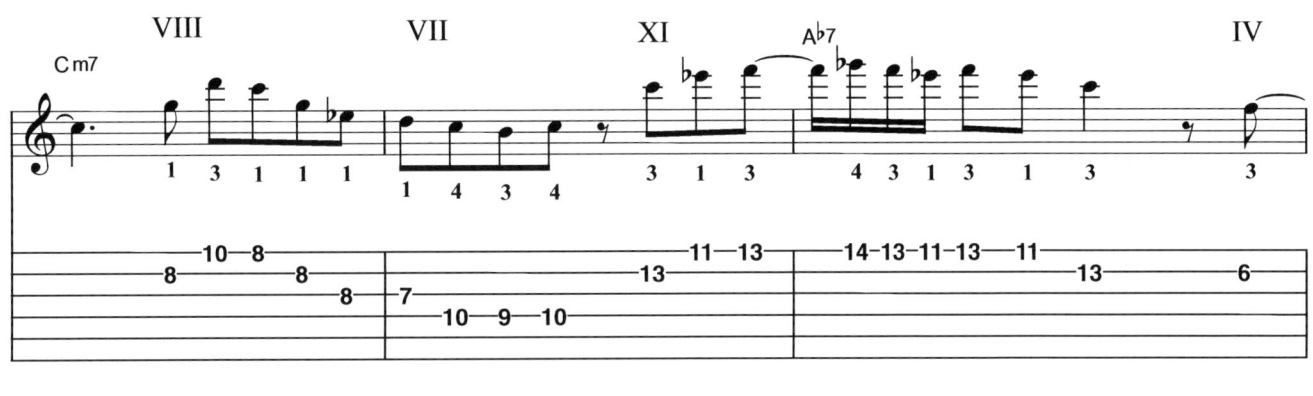

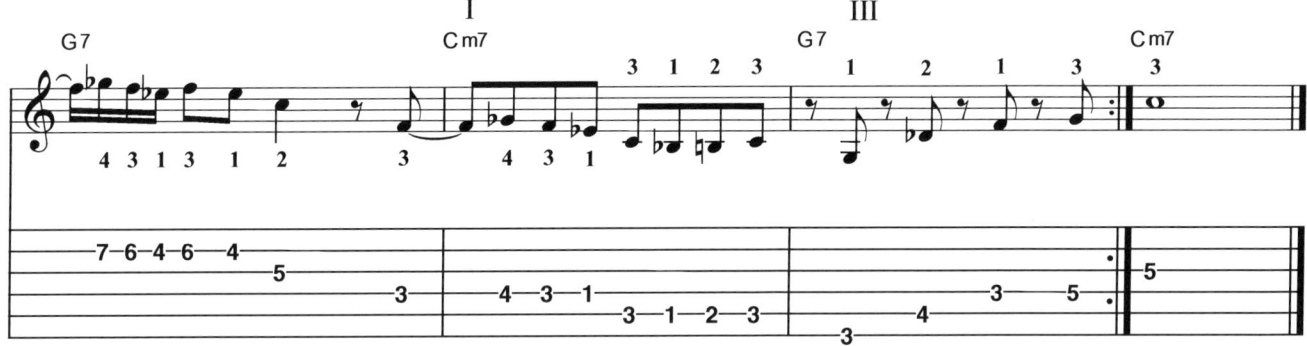

Write Your Own Minor Blues Warm-Up

About the Author

Known as the Dean of New Mexico jazz guitarists, Michael Anthony lives, teaches, and performs in Albuquerque and Santa Fe — traveling often to Los Angeles to perform with friends and colleagues where he was a studio musician throughout the 1960s and 70s.

His credits include touring with Andy Williams, Henry Mancini, and Michele Legrand, to name a few, and long tenure with the orchestras of "The Carol Burnnett Show" and "The Flintstones," among many other network television shows (e.g., Barbara Streisand, Dean Martin, Sonny and Cher). In addition, He worked countless sessions at the major recording studios for the likes of Burt Backarach ("Raindrops Keep Fallin' on My Head"), and Diana Ross ("Theme from Mahogany"). Jazz performances include appearing with Quincy Jones, Blue Mitchell, Ray Brown, Louie Belson, and Gil Evans (accompanying Miles Davis at the 1965 Monterey Jazz Festival).

At sixteen Anthony was already passionately dedicated to the guitar, copying difficult licks from Les Paul's, Barney Kessel's, Tal Farlow's and other guitarists' recordings, leading to lessons and the formal study of music in college, The mentors who influenced Anthony most, however, were Howard Roberts and Joe Pass. It was an early recording session with Roberts that led to Anthony's studio career.

Anthony applies his talent and experience as a guitarist and educator in classes and workshops at both the secondary and university levels, heading up jazz guitar studies at the University of New Mexico.

His discography includes five CD's the most recent being *New Journey* with his Natural Instincts Trio (Lone Guitar Publishing, 2004, www.michaelanthonyonline.com).

Other Mel Bay Books by Michael Anthony

Extreme Warm-Ups and Chops Builders for Guitar (30510)
    Ebook (30510EB)

The Ultimate Map for Jazz Guitar (22037)
    Ebook (22037EB)

WWW.MELBAY.COM

Printed in Great Britain
by Amazon